Hexagonal Graph Notebook

for gamers, quilters
and other crazy people

This book belongs to:

_____

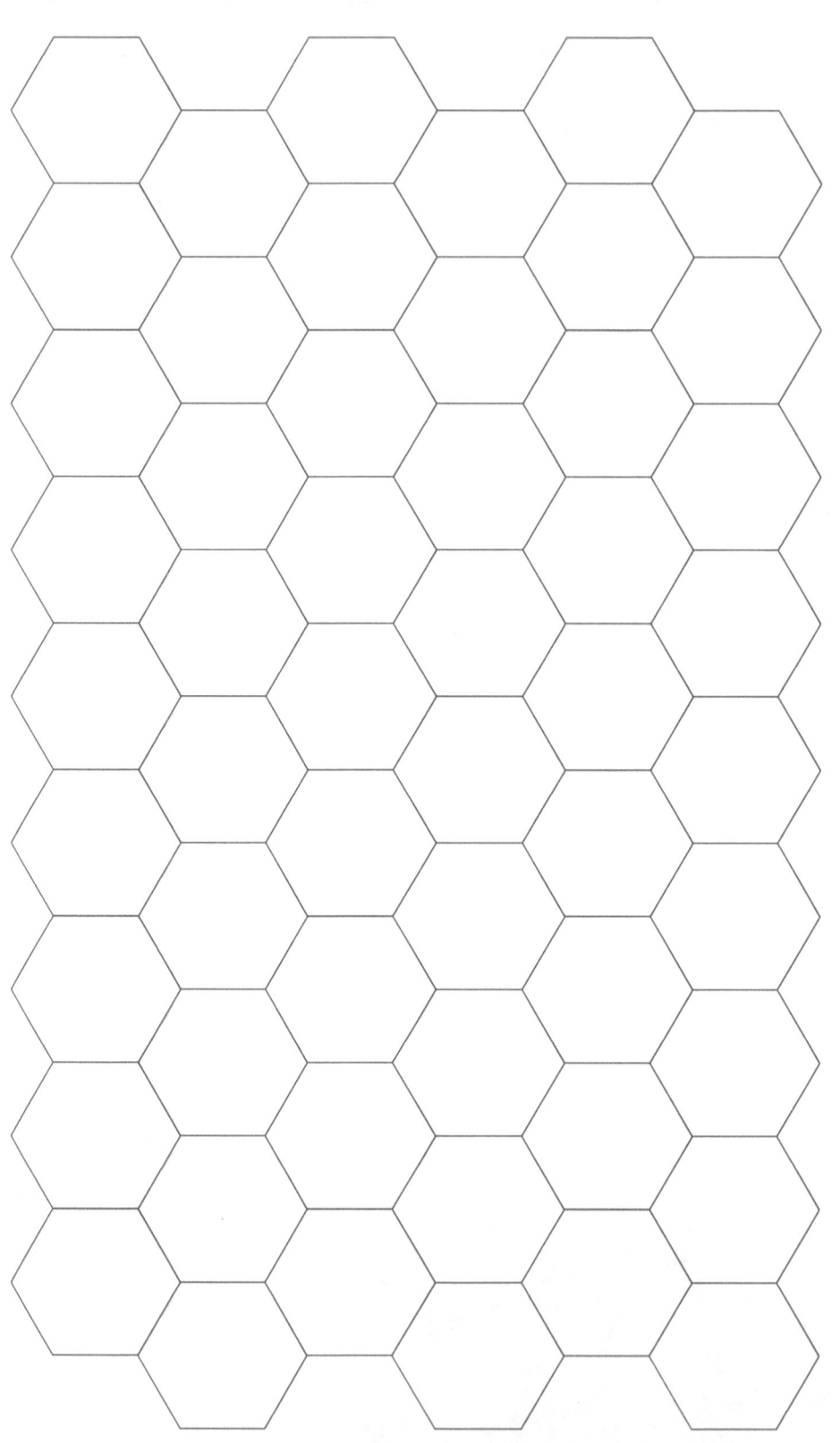

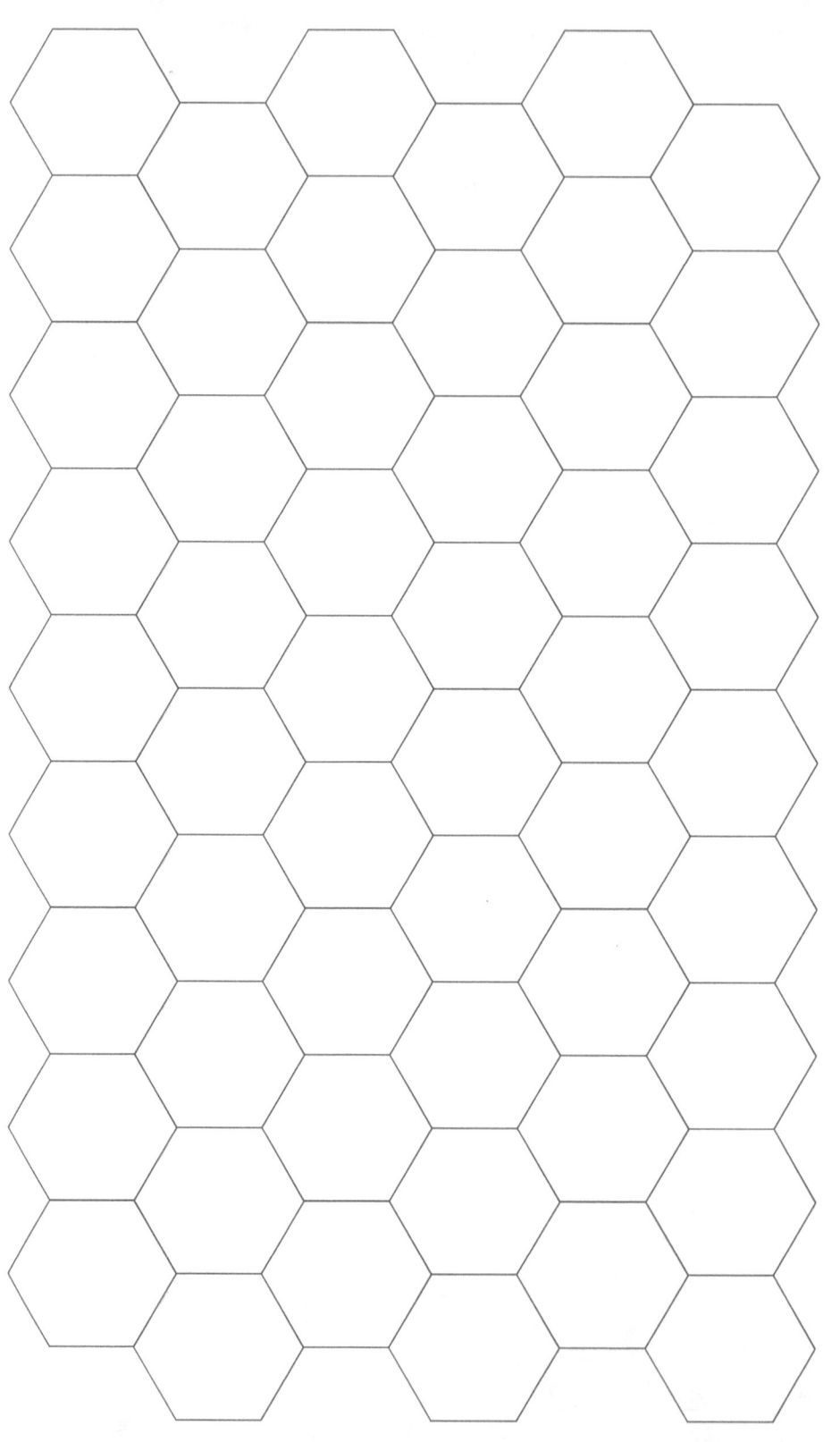

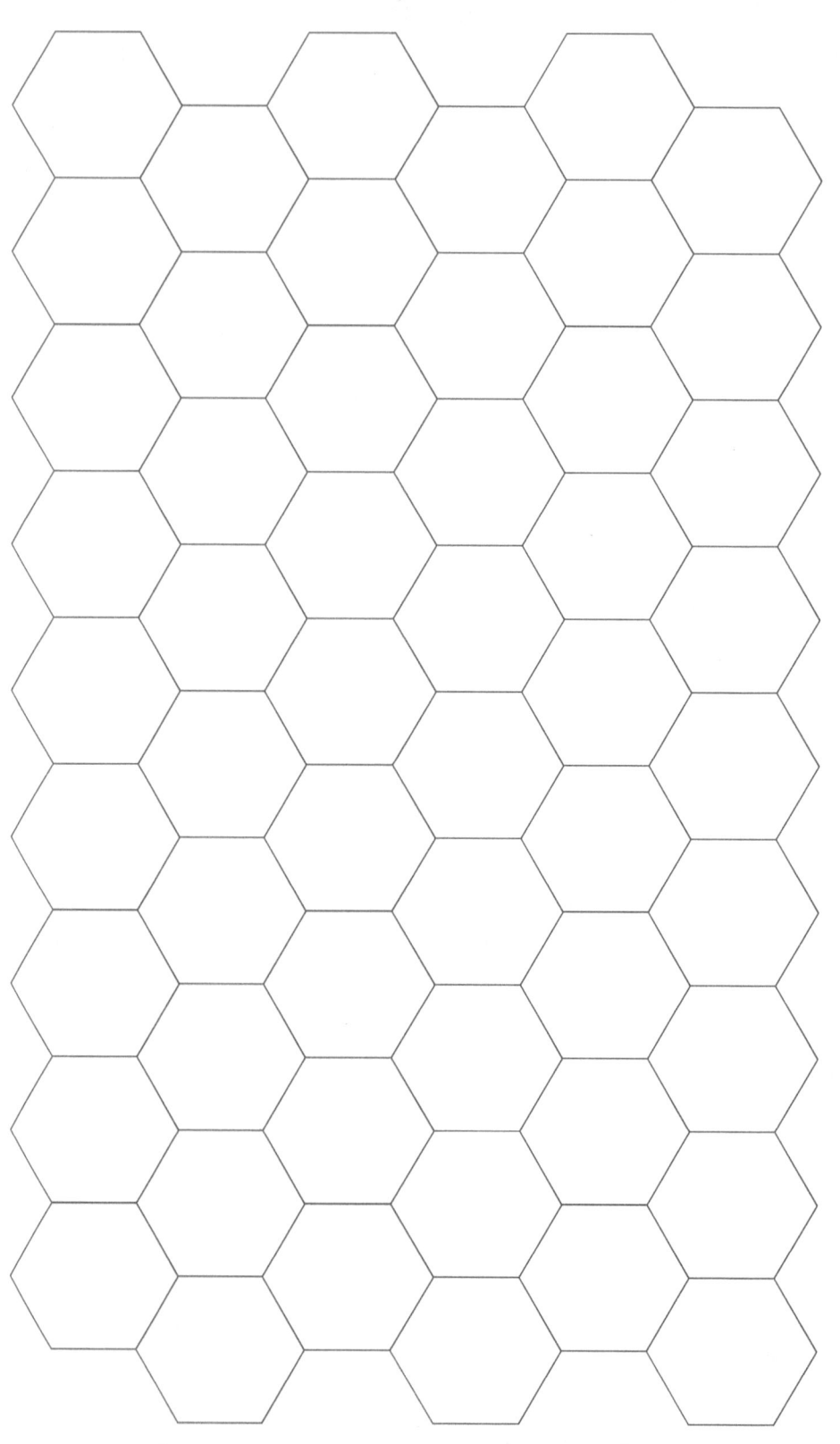

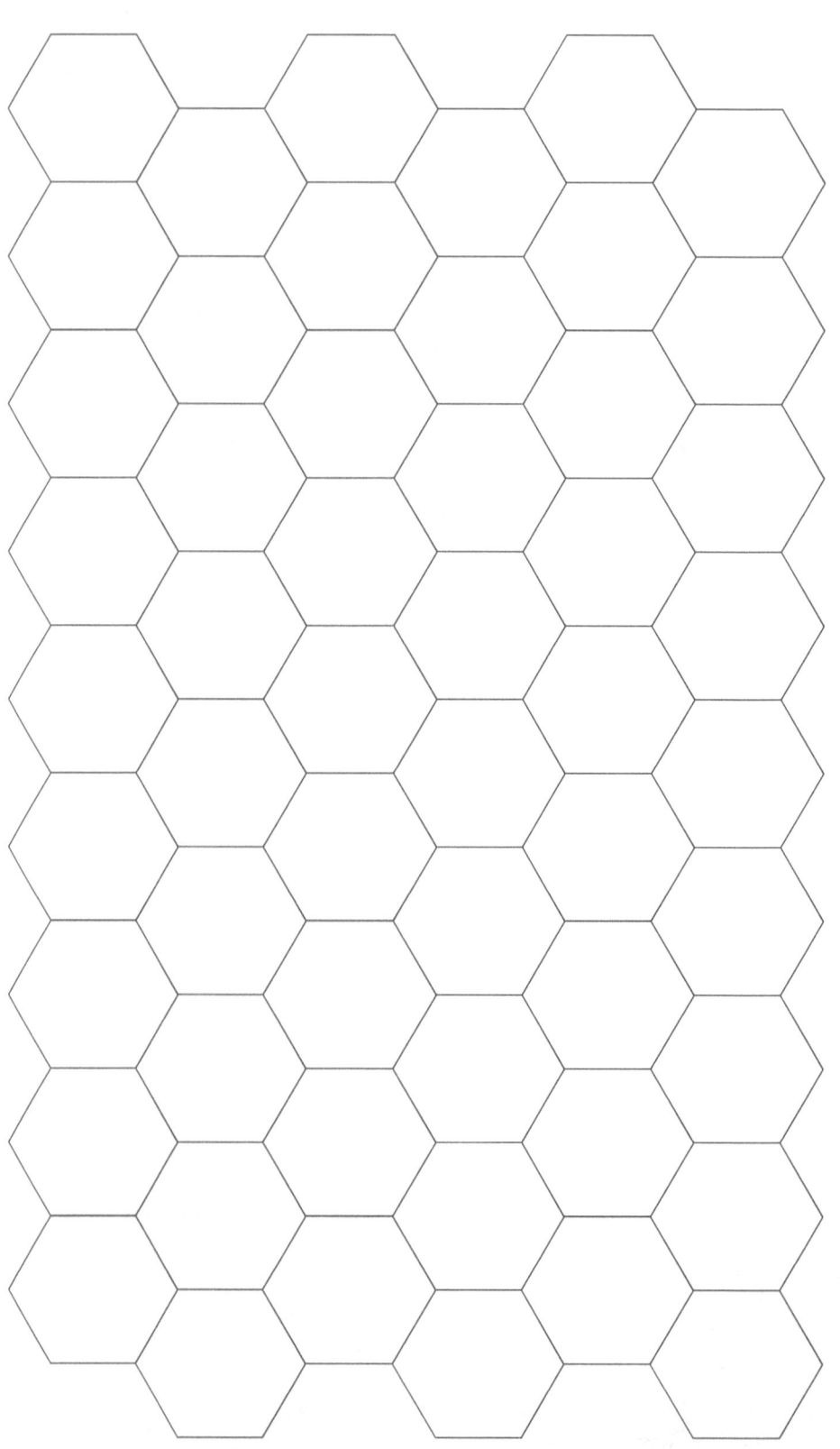

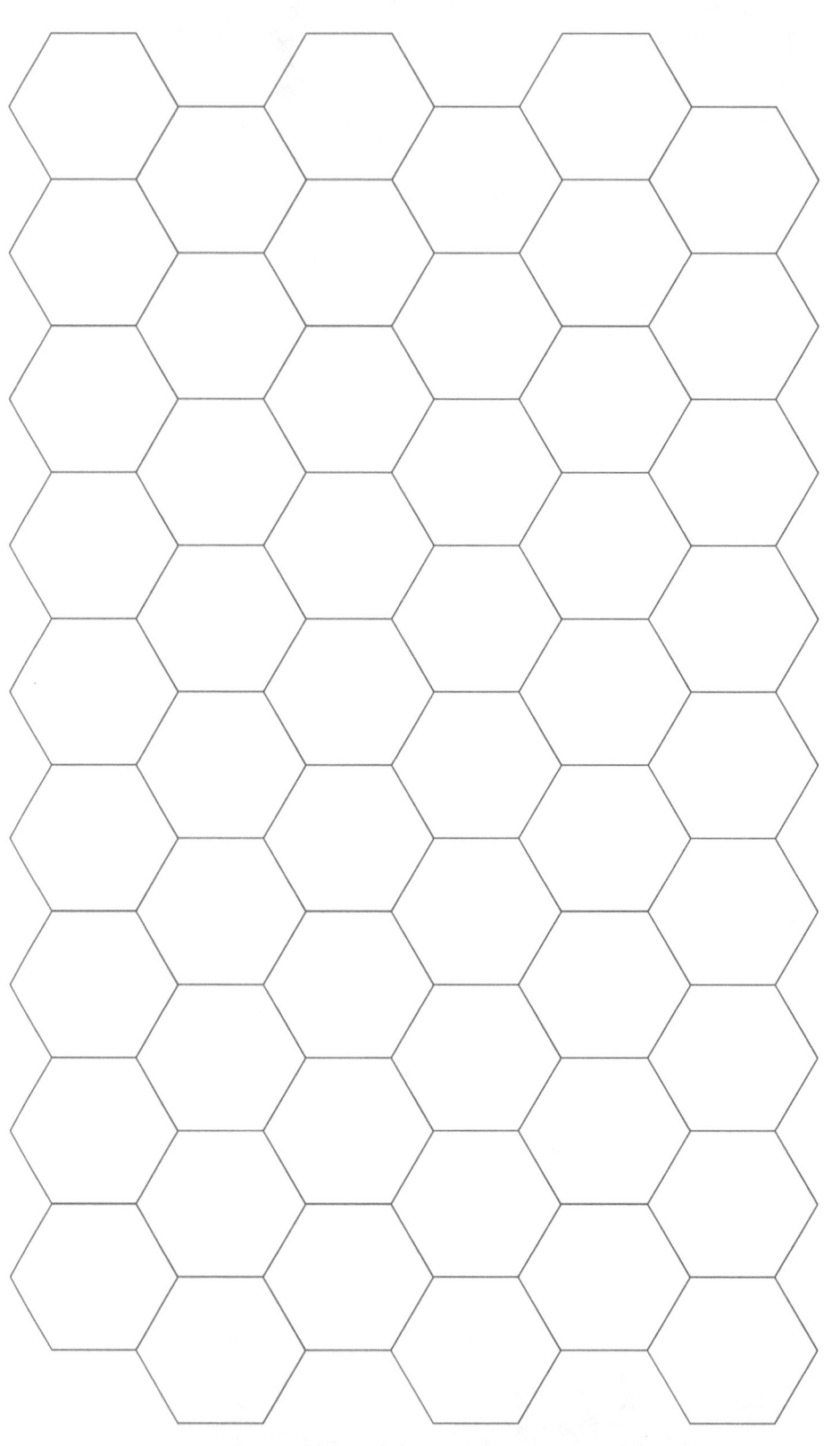

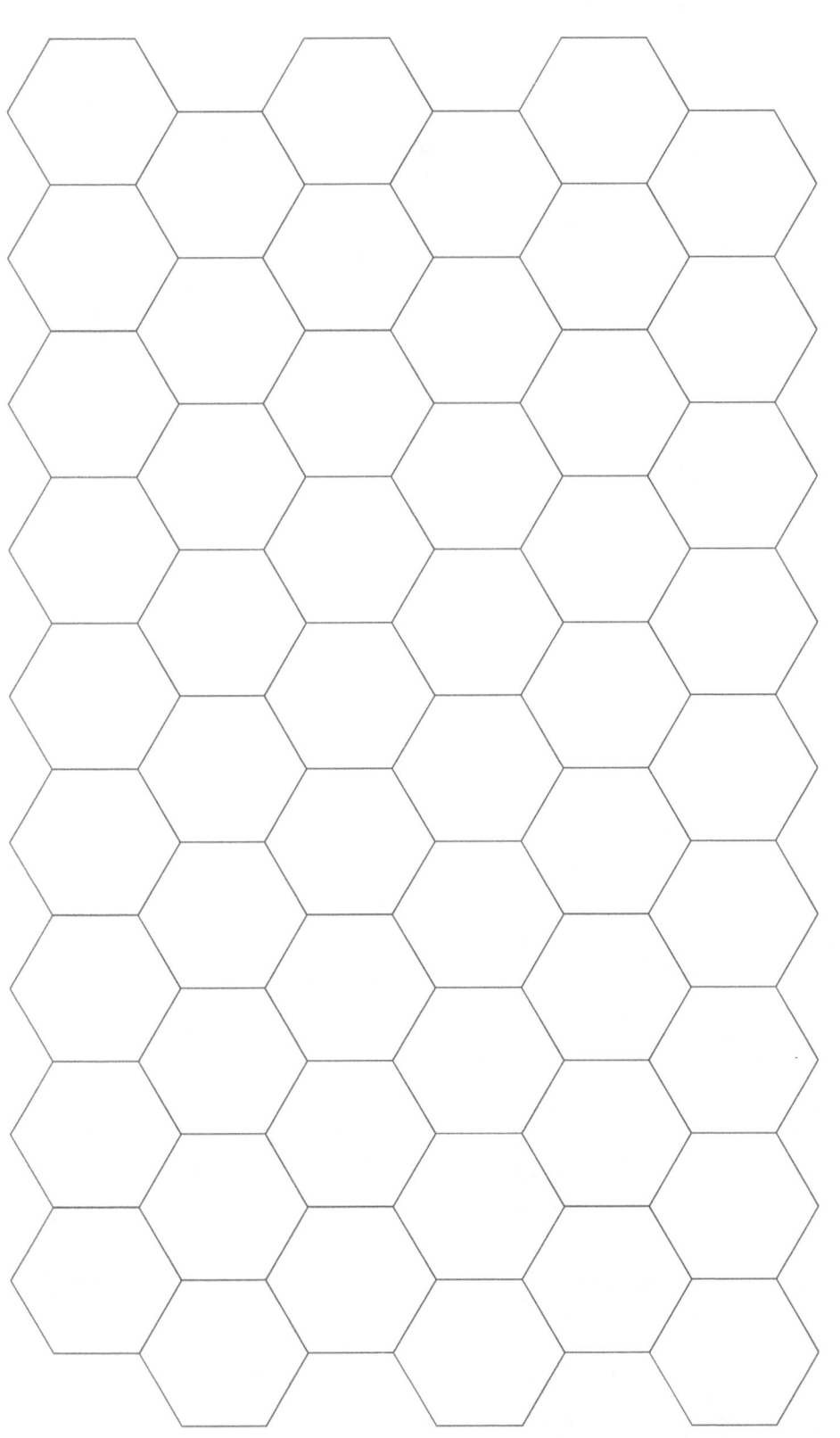

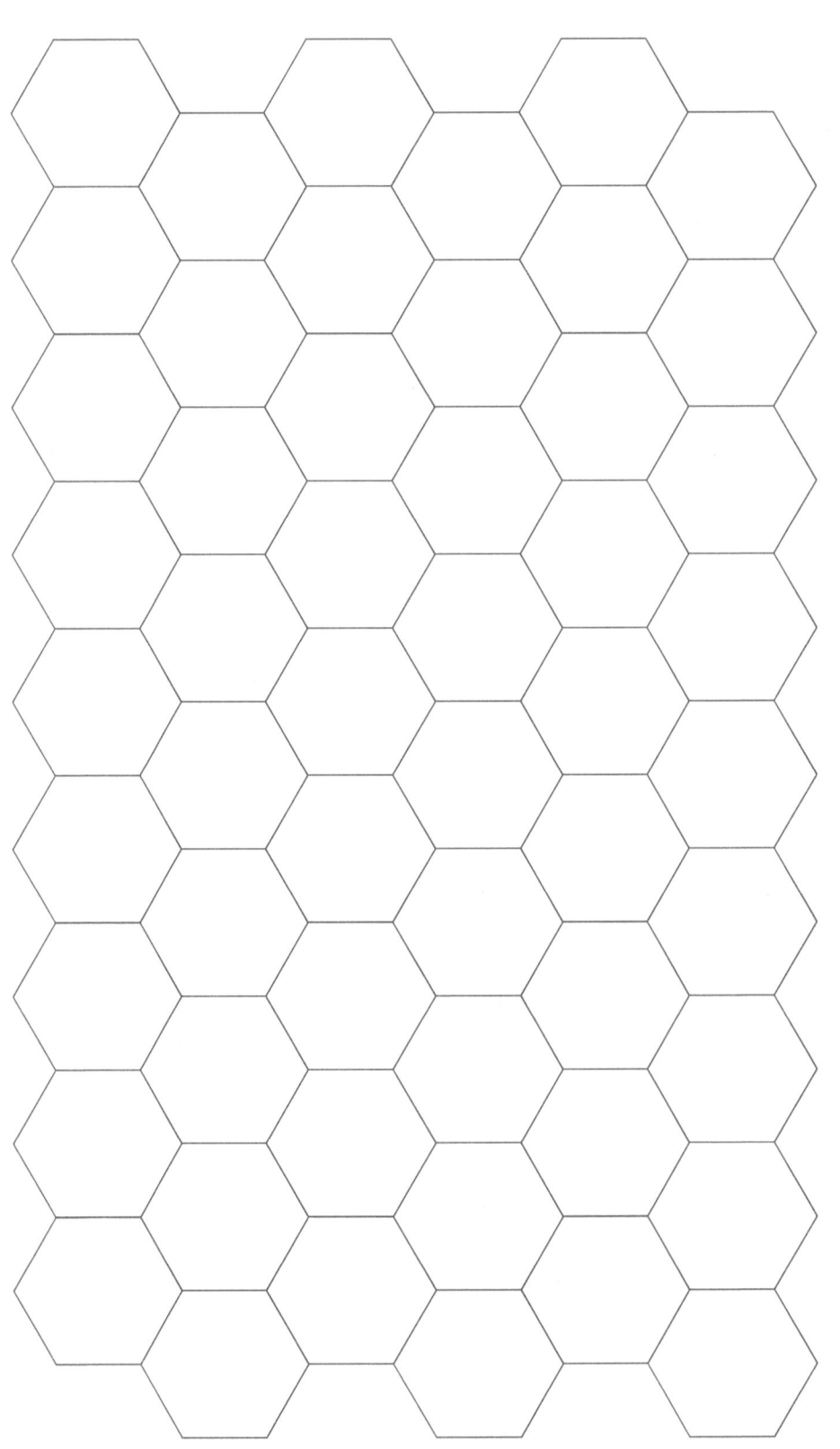

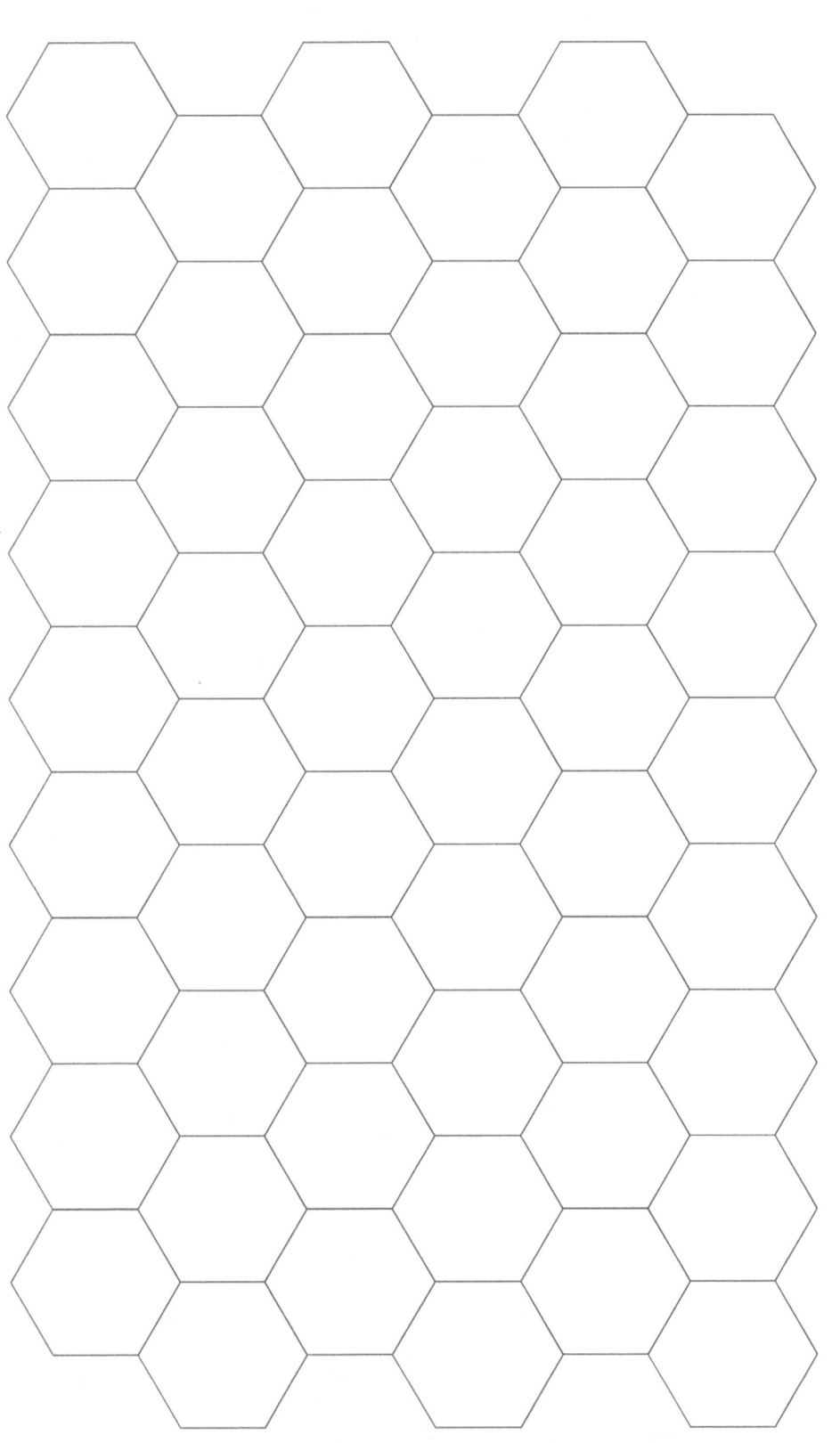

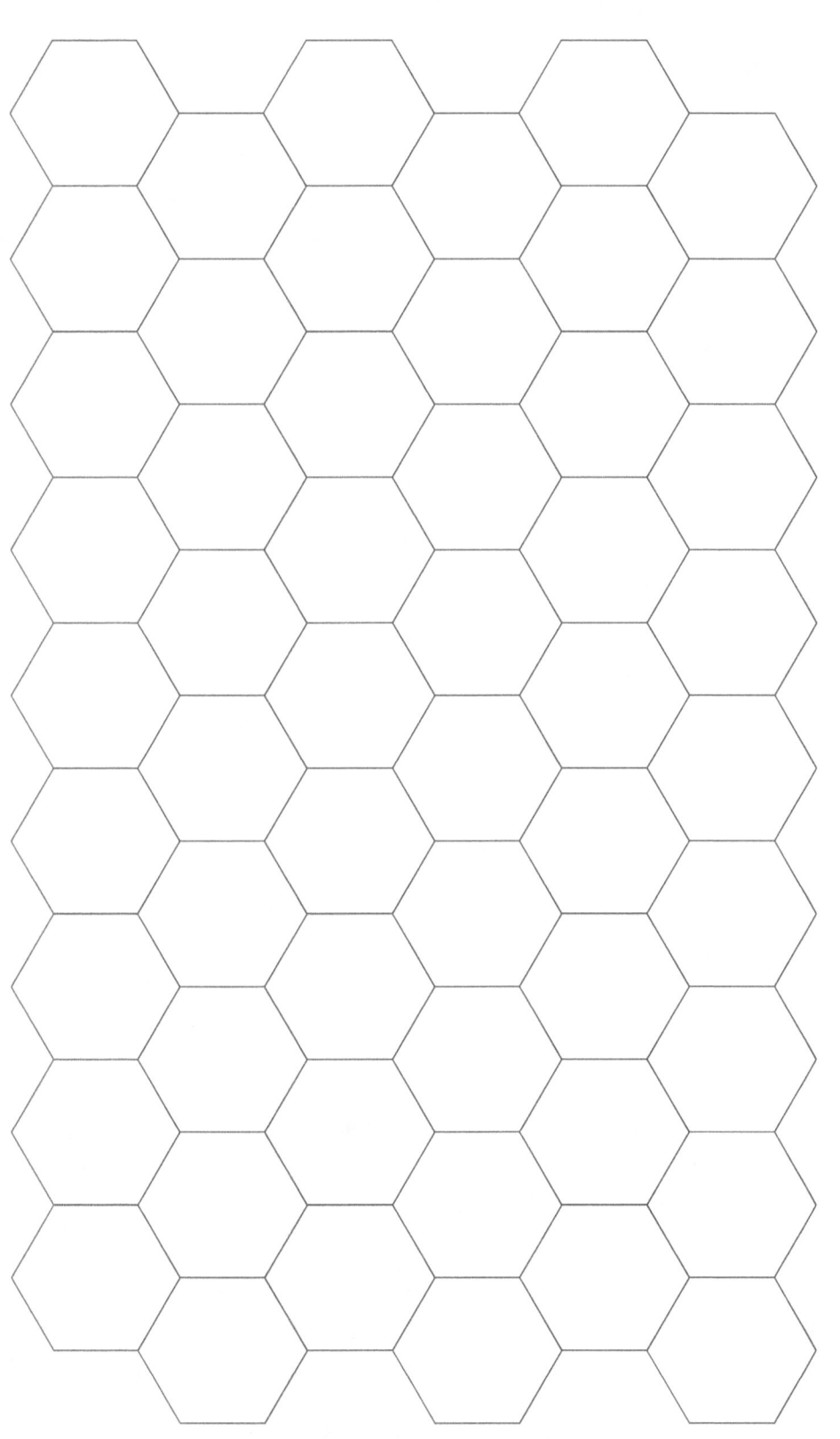

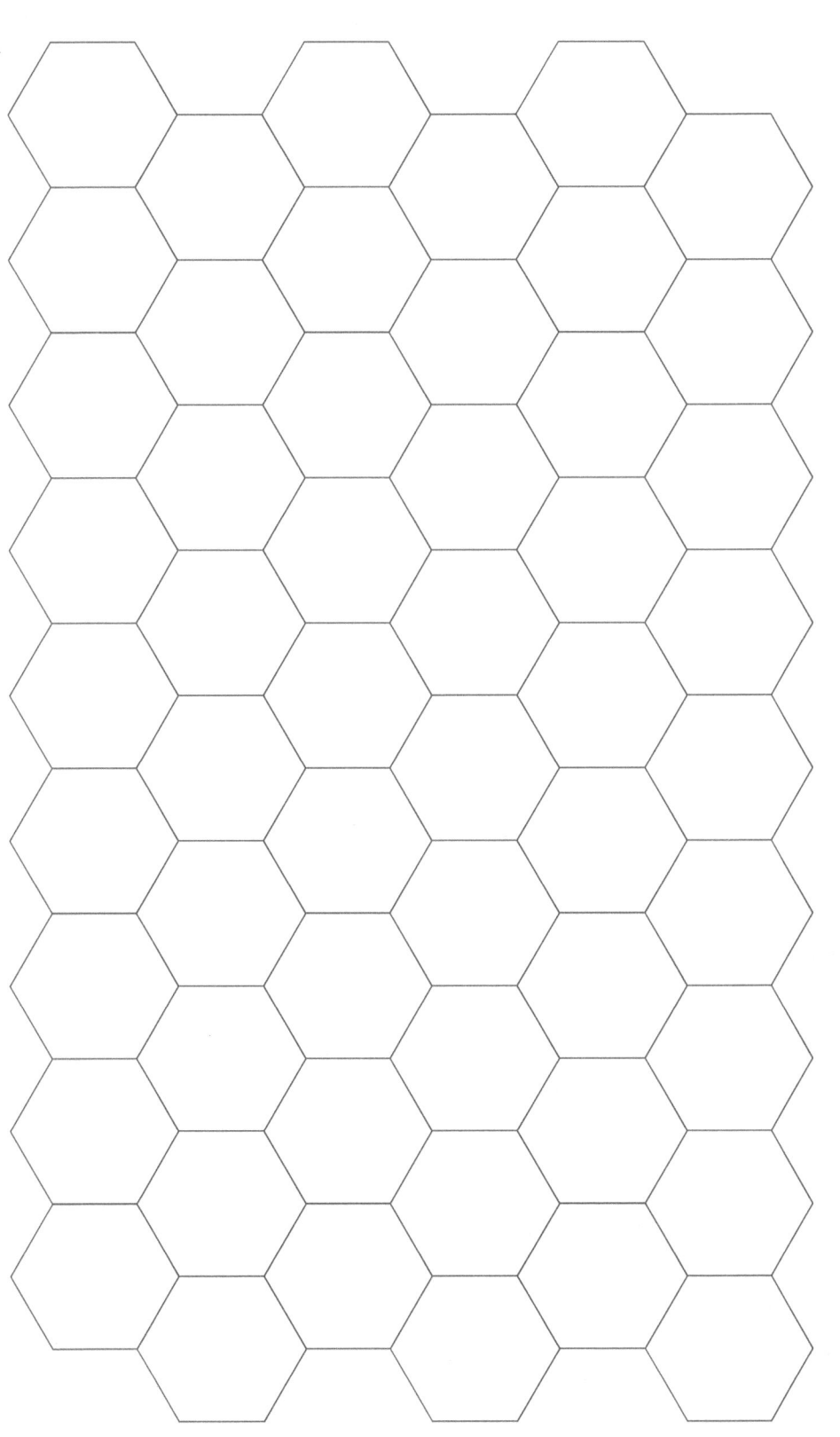

www.ingramcontent.com/pod-product-compliance
Lightning Source LLC
Chambersburg PA
CBHW021836170526
45157CB00007B/2813